THE STAR SHINES IN DARK

IRTIKA MEHRAJ

ISBN 979-888521753-8

Contents

About The Author

Irtika Mehraj

I am IRTIKA MEHRAJ, born on 5 june 2009. I am in class 7th, I am 12 years old, I am from KHREW Dist. PULWAMA (J&K).

I am fond of listening and writing stories which gives the message of motivation and creates enthusiasm. From my childhood my life was full of chaos and full of

suffering and sometimes used to affect me but slowly I learnt and realized the meaning of life. I am not that much intelligent to teach others but. I am a beginner and learner and I will learn till my death.

Whatever my life is hard or easy I have learnt to play with great attitude. Whatever I have lost or whatever I have today is all by the grace of almighty. His choice is always great and whatever he has given me is much for me (ALHAMDULILAH).

I thank Allah who gives me strength to face day to day life and I thank all those who support me in my life.

My dream to do great in life and I will work hard. (INSHAALLLAH).

insta ID- irtika_mehraj

sister insta ID- ameen_amin000

Author's Notes!

I want to give a message of hard work and never to give up in life. Up downs always come in life but we must be consistent to our destination.

Many things keep motivates me in my life. There is no doubt that a person gets lot of pain in suffering but we must take everything as a test and we should play our part whole heartedly.

I have learnt to make things easy, it's possible only when we are happy inside. Happiness lies in everything, depends upon a person's perception. Life is easy if we are happy and satisfied inside.

Here I want to thank those who supports me and motivates me in my life and the person who supports me to complete this book is the most important person of my life. Without this person I am nothing and with this person I am everything. The person is my best friend, my teacher, my mentor and my well-known sister.

Thank you so much my dear sister AMINA MEHRAJ, (coauthor IMPERFECTIONS, THE SUNSHINE AND THE SURPRISE book).

Thank you for being always here to support me, to motivate me and to encourage me.

CHAPTER ONE

Thoughts

LIFE:

Life is a beautiful journey it came once and not again.

It may seem easy but it is very difficult.

Because this life shows us many problems and sufferings. And sometimes this life makes us happy, sometimes it makes us sad.

But in order to fulfill our dreams and move forward in life, we have to face these difficulties.

Life is hard but we make it easy. Learn to live your life happily and Don't be sad when you are in any trouble, Turn your pain into power, strength and passion.

Keep smile everyday, stay strong, live peaceful.

Live your life as you wish but without any mistake. Play with difficulties with your great attitude. And don't be dependent.

We have got this life; this life is very special for us. And life is precious for everyone so learn to live in it.

We need Hard work in our life:

A person needs hard work in his/her life.

It takes hard work to make your dreams come true.

It takes hard work to move forward in life.

Even a person needs hard work to achieve anything.

By working hard, we succeed in our life and we achieve our destination.

Hard work never wastes for anyone.

Remember these words:

1. Think positive.
2. Don't be afraid.
3. Trust yourself.
4. Never give up.
5. Create passion in yourself.
6. Keep trying.
7. Choose your success.
8. Make your dreams in reality, and fulfill your dreams

True love with nature:

1. Rain: The stubble rain playfully bounced off the roof of her umbrella. As she heard the sound of rain, she forgot all her sorrows and slowly she started falling in love with nature.
2. Sky: When I am alone, I look up at the sky and I feel very happy. Blue sky and white clouds, I am singing and walking around.
3. Birds: The birds are chirping in the morning and it seems that they are all singing a song to each other.
4. Garden springs: It's fun to go to the garden in the morning, when I look at the leaves of trees, dew drops fall on them, it looks like they are shining like pearls.

CHAPTER TWO

HOW SHE FORGOT HER DREAMS

There was a girl with beautiful dreams and lot of desires, her parents were poor so she was living with her uncle and he was supporting her and her family. She was very happy and living a peaceful life like princess. She was getting everything that she wished.

As time passed and she grew up, she was without tension as had that person in her life which could bring ocean stars for her and he supported her in every walk of life.

One day she fell ill suddenly. She was then 11. She used to get pain and tears in eyes continuously. She took appointment to a doctor and started to take medicines. After one year there was no affect in her illness. Finally, doctor advised her for eye surgery. She was 12 years old when she had eye surgery and after one-month surgery, suddenly her uncle got heart stroke and he died. She couldn't believe on it and she got depressed. It took a lot of time to realize her that everyone has to die one day but she was still thinking about her uncle's sudden death. Before his uncle's death, he told her that you have to be topper your class. She started to focus on this saying and did not want to break her promise.

After result she really was a topper but was not happy at all as she had lost that person who showed her the world. But when she moved forward in life it was very difficult for her to choose way as she was without support now. Even after having surgery, she was still ill. She was very depressed. She used to remain sad and was broken completely. She used to remain always in deep thinking and was nit talking to anyone. She neither care about herself nor others.

As time passed, she became very ill

She went to doctor and he said that the while surgery the doctor forgot to remove the tube that he had fixed in her eye. She suffered a lot and couldn't focus even on studies. She left all hope.

Finally, the doctor removed the tube, now she got rid from illness. Her family was also suffering because they were poor.

When she started to face the world, to handle day to day situations. She slowly healed from depression. Day to day issues and sufferings of others realized her the reality of life and she learnt that everything is going for a reason and all this is life. She started to motivate herself and thought that life is not easy, its full of miseries; but we have to make it east by our efforts, by our actions.

Now she started finding happiness in everything even in little things. She found happiness in talking with God, watching others laughing, finding herself in a better way to do whatever she wants, observing the creation of God, seeing birds flying in the sky, days and nights, in everyday challenges.

All these started to give her peace and happiness. She started to remain happy whatever she has and started to take responsibility of her family. After these, she completely forgets her dreams and whatever happened to her, whatever she lost. She is no more worried about that and now little things are the causes of her happiness.

She started working as an entrepreneur at small age and continued to study. She has no more desires and she don't want anything from God except peace and happiness. Finally, she left everything on God.

CHAPTER THREE

Miserable life of a girl

Once there was a girl named Aliza living in a small village. She was 13 years old. She was living with her father in an old house. Her father's name was MR. jack. They were very poor. Aliza was very fond of studies and there was no school available in this village.

One day Aliza asked her father," Father, I want to go to school because I want to study because it is my heart's desire,"

Her father replied," I am so sorry but this is not possible."

Aliza asked," why this is not possible." Father replied, "Because school is very far, in city and I can't afford its expanses as I have not much money, so sorry." Aliza asked," what to do with the money."

Father replied, "If you want to go to school in city, we need money which we do not have."

Then Aliza got sad and went to her room.

When Mr. Jack went to his daughter's room, he saw her crying. He thought that he should do something to make money and then send her daughter to school.

Mr. Jack said to his daughter, "I have some work to do, I'll be back in the evening, don't go out of the home and stay indoor."

Aliza didn't answer to her father, and she didn't even look at his father. M.R jack went out of the house. M.R jack wandered here and there in search of job. Suddenly It began to rain and lightning thunder.

Aliza was waiting for her father, gradually she became frightened because it was getting dark. Aliza opened the window of her room and she looked up at the dark sky she felt good, she closed her eyes and said, "I have full confidence in myself, one day I will succeed in my life." And she prayed for herself.

Now M.R jack was back to home, Aliza saw that her father's clothes were wet from the rain she told her father to change his clothes as soon as possible or he may catch a cold.

She saw tears welling up in her father's eyes. Aliza asked her father," that why are you crying." Father replied," I was looking for a good job from which I could earn money but I did not get any job." Aliza said," if you don't stop crying otherwise, I will cry too and you need rest, you go to sleep," Now Aliza put a sheet over his father and he fell asleep. Then Aliza fell asleep in her room.

That night, Mr. Jack's condition worsened, Mr. Jack's brain was affected by too much thinking and he was worried about Aliza. Suddenly he started shouting and his condition got worse. Aliza heard that voice of his father and she hurried to her father. Aliza was scared and there was no one around to help her, Aliza began to cry and ran for help, she reached a great distance and saw a man walking on the road she called the man. The man looked at her and hurried towards her, the man said, "What are you doing here this time?"

Aliza replied, “My father’s condition has deteriorated, I saw you here, will you help us?’

The man replied, “What happened to your father?” Aliza said, “I don’t know. Please Come with me and see what has happened to him.” The man said yes, let’s hurry. The man saw Mr. Jack who was in a really very bad condition.

The man said to Aliza, “I have to take your father to the hospital.” Aliza said yes let’s go, Then the man brought his car and they got out of there. Now they have reached the hospital, Now the man has taken MR. jack inside the hospital, the doctor began checking up on Mr. Jack.

The doctor said Mr. Jack had a very bad heart attack. Now we have to treat it as soon as possible.

Aliza started crying and she got scared. She told the doctor to treat her father quickly and if something happens to her father, she can’t live without her father. The doctor replied, “Let’s see what happens. We will try and treat your father. Now you stop crying.” Now Mr. Jack has been shifted to the ward. Now The man said to Aliza, “Dear, you need rest. Let’s go to home now.” Aliza said, “I will go out of the hospital when my father’s condition improves.”

The man said, “I know you are very sad.’ Come on, I swear we will be back tomorrow, if you don’t take care of yourself, then who will take care of your father? Come on you need rest.”

Aliza said,” let’s go but tomorrow morning we will come back soon.” The man said “ok let’s go dear.”

The man was very kind hearted and he took Aliza to his house. The man said to Aliza, “sleep on my bed. I will sleep on the floor today.” Aliza said, “I have a habit of sleeping on the floor." The man told Aliza to obey the elders. Aliza said ok.

Aliza couldn't sleep all night. She was thinking about her father and she was crying a lot. It was six o'clock in the morning, Aliza open her eyes and she got up quickly. She hurried out and went to the man and said we have to go to the hospital quickly. The man said yes, let's go, and before that, eat some food so that you don't feel hungry on the way. She said, "I am not hungry. I have to go to my father soon." Then they both got out of there, and They both reached the hospital. Aliza saw the doctor and she ran to him. She said, "Is my father well?" The doctor said, "Now your father is out of danger. You can see him, but don't talk to him for too long.

Aliza was very happy and she said to the doctor, thank you for healing my father, then she hurried to her father. The doctor said, "Daughter, it was my duty." Aliza reached her father. When Mr. Jack looked his daughter, he said, "Come to me quickly." Aliza hurried to her father and hugged him, and she said, "Daddy, let's go home quickly. And if something happened to you, what would I do alone in this world? Mr. Jack said to his daughter: I will not leave you, and I have no one in this world without you. Aliza said, "You are fine now. This is the biggest thing for me."

Now the doctor came and start talking, MR. jack if You will be fine and if you are feeling well, you can leave here, and take of care of you and your daughter. Mr. Jack said I am fine now and I would like to go my home the doctor said, "All right."

MR Jack thanked the stranger man who had taken him to the hospital on time, the man said, "I don't need you thank you. It was my pleasure.

MR Jack said again, what's your name? And thank you so much for taking care of my daughter, ''The man said,'' I am MR Donald and I have a little hotel in city. I am a manager of that hotel and don't worry Your daughter is also my daughter, and whenever you want to come to my hotel you can I am waiting for you people'' Mr. jack said, "oh, thank you why not we will come to visit".

Now Aliza was very happy and she went home with her father, Mr. Jack said to Aliza, "I will definitely send you to school so when you grow up you can live your life happily. Aliza said, "I don't want to talk about it again because it made your condition worse. I don't want to see you in that condition again, we are just as good as we are".

The father replied," I can't be with you forever because one day I will have to leave this world and you, So I will send you to school and you will have to work hard so that you do not have to suffer after I die.

Only then will my soul find peace". Aliza started crying and said, I am not going anywhere without you and it is my dream to study but it does not mean that you will leave me. I love you so much and please don't leave me alone. The father replied, "If you love me so much, then obey me."

Aliza said, "You need rest. It is late at night I will tell you the answer tomorrow morning." The father said, "Okay, I'll rest now and you can sleep in your room." Good night my dear, Aliza went to her room, she was very upset and she was crying all night., Mr. Jack slowly walked over to her daughter's room and saw that she was crying and he began to cry a lot He thought, I don't want my daughter to give up in her life and I will surely let her to study. Then he went to his room

It will be morning now, and Aliza was ready to give answer to her father, she went to her father's room. When Aliza reached her father's room, her father was not present in the room. Then Aliza went outside and her father was sitting outside in the courtyard. Aliza went to her father and said, "I want to talk to you." The father replied, "I can't change my mind. I haven't heard anything." Aliza says again, I want to say the same thing, now I will obey you". Father said," I know you are my good daughter and I was sure you would obey me.

Aliza said, "Daddy, should we prepare to go out?" The father replied, "I am not coming with you. You are going alone." Aliza was shocked and said," how can I go to there alone and this is what you are telling me? The father said, "I want you to learn to live without me from today." And I will leave you there and then I will come back in village. ''Aliza said how can you take me away from yourself And I'm not going anywhere without you".

The father said, "Now listen to me, Let's get ready to go out and pack your bag". Aliza couldn't believe what was happening. She went to her room, Mr. Jack went to the back of his house and he sat there. He started crying and started talking to himself "I did not want to do this but I am compelled. I want my daughter to hate me more from today and after my Death she will not remember me. Now Mr. Jack called his daughter and said," hurry up, it's getting late".

Now Aliza came out and she took her father's hand and said," let's go, it's getting late. A vehicle was coming on the way and they both got into it and reached the city. Aliza asked her father on the way," I have a question for you, can you give me the answer"?

Father said why not, Aliza said," if you didn't even get a job then where will you get the money and how will I study without money"? The father replied, "Don't worry, I have found a good job. Whenever you need money, I will send you money from the village to city and sometimes I will come to see you".

Aliza said," it's good that you got a job, but what kind of job is that?

Father replied," don't pay attention there, that's a good job for me". Aliza said, ok fine".

Father said," remember my last words to work hard in your life, to move forward in your life, and never give up and u have to stay in a hotel". Aliza said, "where is that hotel? Father said,' The manager of that hotel is MR Donald, Aliza said," oh, that uncle, he is very kind hearted".

Aliza said to her Father, now I want to ask you one last question, "why you will not stay with me"? And why you will leave me alone? The father replied," if I stayed here with you, where would the money for your education come from? So, I will live in the village and earn money from there".

Aliza said, "Now you have got a job and I am very happy. If you had told me earlier, I would not have been so angry and now I will work hard and study hard." The father said you are my good daughter. Let's go inside the hotel., Now they both went inside the hotel to meet MR Donald. The MR Donald saw them both and ran towards them, he said welcome to my little hotel. Aliza said thank you. "Mr. Jack told MR Donald "I'm leaving my daughter to you. Take good care of my daughter." Donald replied don't worry your daughter is also my daughter". Mr. Jack hugged his daughter and said, "I'm leaving and take care of yourself.", Aliza started crying and said, I will miss you very much". Father said, I will miss you too my sweet queen". Then Mr. Jack left the hotel.

Aliza said to Mr. Donald, "uncle, where is my room, where I can keep my belongings"? MR Donald replied, "I have already prepared a nice room for you, and that room is upstairs." Aliza picked up her luggage and went upstairs. Today was Eliza's first day at school and she is very happy, when she arrived inside the school, she was surprised because the school was so big and beautiful. She went to her class and saw that there were many children there and she was very happy that she would get to talk to them now. These children saw Aliza and they started talking. "Sit here, you are our new friend" Aliza said, "Thank you all".

A teacher came to this class. He saw that new students have come to this class today. The teacher told Aliza to stand up and introduce yourself. Aliza stood up and started talking.

"My Name is Aliza, I am 13 years old. And I am from village". The teacher said, "you are a good girl". Now all students clapped for her. Aliza said' "thank you teacher". Teacher said, "now sit down"., Aliza was very happy and her first day of school went very well.

There, in the village, Mr. Jack is cleaning a hospital and talking to himself, I didn't tell my daughter what I am doing because she would be very upset if I told her that I was doing the cleaning in hospital".

Today is Eliza's class test, and she is studying hard. Now Aliza came to school fully prepared and her paper started. She wrote answers to all the questions. And she got full marks and she was very happy. And she became impatient and said, "When my father sees my Marks, he will be very happy." Now MR Donald came to Aliza and said, to her, "If you are hungry, come to me and I will give you food. Then you can eat in your room." Aliza said, "I am very happy today. I have something to say to you and you listen to me quickly." MR Donald said, "Dear, tell me what's the matter." Aliza said today was my class test and I got full marks. He said, "Wow, that's a good thing Congratulations dear''. Aliza said, thank you so much uncle.

3 months later, Aliza became very upset and wondered why my father did not come to see me. He promised me that I would come, but why did he not come now? What's the matter, I think my father is in big trouble, Or I think my father got sick. No, no what I'm thinking is wrong, I think my father will have some work to do and that is why he is not coming to see me". Now Aliza left her room, and she started looking for Uncle Donald. She saw uncle Donald sitting outside the hotel and then she went outside.

Aliza said to uncle Donald from a distance, "I have something important to say to you." MR Donald replied, "yes my dear come here and tell me what are you saying? Aliza said, "uncle Donald Come with me. I want to ask you something If you don't mind" MR Donald replied' "yes why not". Aliza said, "I am feeling very strange. I don't know why.'' MR Donald said, "Are you all right? Why do you look weird? What's bothering you?" Aliza said," I am worried because I thought my father is in trouble. I'm very much worried about my father and my father promised me that he would come to see me, but why didn't he come? Can you please tell me why my father didn't meet me"? MR Donald said, "dear no problem don't get tense I think your father will have some important work so he did not come to see you otherwise he will come, and you're father loves you so much and tomorrow morning I will go to the village ,Aliza said," if you have to go to the village then I will come with you. MR Donald replied," No you can't come with me because you have to go to school and you don't have to miss any school day, you pay attention to your studies, And I promise you, tomorrow I'll bring your father here with me. Be happy, keep relax and now go to your room". Aliza said, "Yes, that's right."

Aliza was very impatient, and she was waiting for the morning when she would meet to her father. MR Donald has brought food for Aliza and said, let's eat quickly then go to sleep because tomorrow morning you have to go to school early. Aliza said," uncle did you forgot, tomorrow I have to meet my father", MR Donald replied, "Yes, I remember that you have to meet your father tomorrow. Now Let's be happy and finish your dinner quickly".

It would be morning now. Aliza got up quickly. Aliza hurry to Uncle Donald and she said loudly," do you remember you have to go to the village today and bring my father here". MR Donald laughed and said, "yes dear I know, now let's go to school. Aliza was very happy. She said," I will come back from school soon and then I will meet my father".MR Donald was getting ready to go to the village he got out of city and got on the village bus. Now MR Donald reached the village and they started looking for MR Jack. Now MR Donald went to Mr. Jack's house. But Mr. Jack was not there. Now Mr. Donald saw a man on the way. Mr. Donald went to the man and asked him, if I could ask you something? Strange man said' yes why not. Mr. Donald's spoke to the man. There was a man in the house whose name was Mr. Jack. Do you know him? Can you tell me where he is? The man said, "Why are you looking for him?" Mr. Donald said, "he is my special friend and I have come to see him." The man said, "It's a pity you came too late." Mr. Donald said, "Why are you saying this? Why am I late?" The man replied," the man you are talking about is no more". Mr. Donald said to the man, "You look like you're lying. You don't know the man I'm talking about." The man said, "If you don't trust me, go to where he worked and ask the people where he is." Mr. Donald asked the man," tell me the name of the place where he worked"? The man said, "he was cleaning a hospital and I had seen him work there many times".

Mr. Donald arrived at the hospital he saw the doctor and called him. The doctor came to Mr. Donald and said," yes what's the matter". MR Donald told the doctor that there was a man at the hospital whose name was MR Jack. Can you tell me where he is? The doctor replied, "Yes, I know that man, but why do you want to know about him?" MR Donald replied," I'm asking you about him because he is a good friend of mine and you can tell me where he is at the moment". The doctor said," you are talking about Mr. Jack but he is no more in this world". Mr. Donald asked the doctor," can you please tell me what had happened to him? was he in any trouble or something else"? The doctor said," one day Mr. Jack came to me and he was saying give me a job in your hospital because I need money, Then I asked him why do you need money". He said," my daughter has to study. I need money for that. Then I will enroll her in city school". Then I told him I can't give you a job here because you're a heart patient and anything can happen to you anytime. But he didn't listen to me. He said I need a job here. Then I was forced to hire him. Then one day Mr. Jack was cleaning and he had a heart attack. We tried very hard to save him but it was impossible to save him. We had already told him that if you had another heart attack. It will be difficult, then he left this world at that time. Mr. Donald was very upset and he started crying a lot. The doctor asked Mr. Donald why are you crying. MR Donald said: "I am crying because I have his little daughter and what shall I say to her now? I have told her daughter that I will bring your father with me but now I don't even deserve to face it.

The doctor said and I remembered one thing Mr. Jack wrote a letter for you and his daughter one day and then he put it to me and said if anything happens to me give it to them. Mr. Donald asked the doctor to give me the letter. The doctor took two letters from his room and handed them to MR Donald. MR Donald wondered if I would first read the letter that Mr. Jack had written for me. Mr. Donald began reading the letter, in which MR jack wrote: "I am leaving my daughter to you. I trust you. You will take good care of my daughter and love her more than me." Mr. Donald started crying and he started thinking what should I say to Aliza and how should I tell her that your father is no more in this world. And if I told her, then how could she bear the pain? Mr. Donald thought, "I'll see what happens now. I'll explain it. And now Mr. Donald left the village and got on the bus to Srinagar. A few hours later, MR Donald reached their hotel. Mr. Donald went to his room and he was waiting for Aliza to come and I will tell her this sad news.

Aliza is very happy in school. She thinks that I will get out of school quickly and meet her father. Aliza get out of school and she started running and she reached the hotel. Now she is impatient that I will go in and hug my father. When she went inside, she saw that no one was there. She began to ask, “Is there anyone here?” And now Aliza went to MR Donald’s room and saw that Uncle Aliza put her school bag down and start talking Uncle Donald what’s the matter. MR Donald stood up and put his hand on Aliza’s head and began to speak, what I am going to tell you I know you will be very sad about this.

Aliza said what you have to say you tell me later but first tell me where my father is, he came with you or not? Mr. Donald replied, “I want to tell you the same thing about your father, and I said, ‘If you have to listen, listen carefully, and I know you’ll be very sad, now whether you are sad or something else I don’t care, I will keep telling you. Aliza said, “Tell me what you have to say.” Mr. Donald said softly, “Your father is no more.” And it’s been a month and I found out today. But at first, I couldn’t believe it, then later the doctor told me everything about your father. I know you won’t believe it but that’s true.

Aliza became silent, she was not saying anything. Mr. Donald said to Aliza, “Why aren’t you talking? I’m talking to you. Aren’t you listening to me? Do you think I’m lying?” Aliza cried and said, “I can’t believe what you are saying, but you can’t say lie to me” Aliza started crying a lot and she started talking to MR Donald, “that’s why my father told me to go to city alone. If I had known, I would not have come here, but what can I do now that they have left me and he promised me that I will not leave you and he broke his promise. Uncle Donald now you tell me how can I live without my father and where would I go and why did he do that and why did he take me away from him”. MR Donald said, “If you are your father’s brave daughter, stop crying.” And your father has written a letter for you. I brought that letter with me. Do you want to read it?

Aliza said, "yes give me that letter and I will read". Mr. Donald handed the letter to Aliza, And Aliza started reading that letter. Mr. Jack wrote in the letter, "Forgive me if you can, my dear daughter, I could not fulfill your dreams but I hope you will work hard and you are my brave daughter and I hope you'll do what I couldn't. I trust you so much that you can live alone, you don't need anyone in your life, you are my good daughter and you study hard and fulfill your dreams. One most important thing, I want to tell you that in your life, never cry in front of anyone and now you have to live your life for yourself and not for anyone else".

Aliza stopped crying and she took a deep breath and she sat down. Mr. Donald asked Aliza, "Did you see now that your father wants you to be brave?" Aliza said, "If my father's soul is happy with my happiness and my hard work, then I will work hard and I will be happy in life." Mr. Donald said' "you are very brave girl. And now you have to work for yourself and your father and get to your destination and Your father has entrusted me with your responsibility and I want to fulfill this responsibility. Just pay attention to your studies and whatever you spend on your studies, I will pay for it myself." "If you succeed in life then I will be very happy and I don't need anything in return and I have no one in this world I don't have a daughter, I consider you my as daughter. You will make your life so beautiful if you work hard for it and I will support you.

Aliza said thank you so much uncle Donald. Mr. Donald said, you don't need to thank me."

Eight years later, Aliza had grown up. And she was preparing for her entrance exams. She also was in charge of the hotel because Mr. Donald couldn't work anymore. He was too old. After some weeks, Aliza's exams were coming up. Aliza manage the hotel from morning till evening and she studied at night. Aliza also cooked and feed Mr. Donald. Mr. Donald said to Aliza "Until yesterday you needed me, but today I need you, and until yesterday I used to feed you, but today you are feeding me." I don't know when you will grow up. And if your father were alive, he would be very happy to see you like this.

Aliza said' that soon I will get success then my father will be very happy and his soul will also find peace. MR Donald said' yes dear you are right. God bless you. Now the exams were coming in two days. Aliza is working hard and she is well prepared for the exams. Aliza was reading in the night. Suddenly she fell asleep. She saw in her dream that her father was calling her and telling her to read well and be happy. Aliza quickly opened her eyes and saw that I was having a dream. Aliza started crying but then she wiped her tears and said I have never cried in my life. Because I promised my father I would never cry.

Aliza went to take exams. A rich man was standing behind Aliza. He asked," can I talk to you? Aliza said, yes sure. This rich man asked Aliza," what are you doing here? Aliza replied, "Why are you asking me this question?" This rich man laughed and said that this exam is only for rich people and not for poor people. Aliza got angry at first, but then she moved from there to another place. The exam had begun. At first Aliza got nervous inside but then she remembered that I have to fulfill my dream. The Aliza arrived in the examination hall she saw that there were a lot of rich people and those rich people were making fun of Aliza. But Aliza ignored them all and sat on her seat. Aliza started giving exams.

Aliza was self-confident and worked hard. After 5hours, the exam was over and everyone went out of the hall. And now Aliza went to the hotel, and went to Mr. Donald. MR Donald asked Aliza, come sit here. Aliza said, “I will clean the hotel first and then I will talk to you.” Mr. Donald said, “I trust you. You will definitely pass the exam. The result will come in a few days.” And don’t worry. hard work never wastes for anyone. Aliza said, “yes I hope”.

After a week, the result was coming and Aliza is very impatient. Now Aliza went to see the result. She saw that the first name on the chart was her and there was no limit of her happiness. She had passed the exam with first rank. She could not believe herself. She hurried to Mr. Donald. When MR Donald heard this, he was very happy and there were tears in his eyes and Aliza also fulfilled her father’s dreams. Now everyone came to meet Aliza and everyone was saying her congratulations. Aliza became a doctor in the hospital where her father worked. After overcoming many difficulties, Aliza succeeded in her life and she did not give up and because of hard work, Aliza succeed in her life.

....Theme! This story shows us that no matter how dark our life is and no matter how difficult and painful life is, but by working hard we find the way automatically and we also find the destination of our life. And the hard work of those who work hard is never be wasted. It is only by working hard that we get what we need in our lives. If we want to move forward in our lives and fulfill our dreams, we must be consistent and our dreams will come true.

CHAPTER FOUR

A driver & his son

One day a boy named KAVIN was living with his father Harry. But KAVIN was an idiot and lazy. Every day, Harry wanted his son to focus on his studies and sometimes to help him. But KAVIN would not listen to his father. 'One day HARRY asked his son that if he could help him and bring him some goods from the market' But KAVIN disobeyed his father and replied, "I am not your servant'. Then Harry bought his goods from the market. The next day, HARRY told his son, that he was going to drive a truck that day and he should take care of the house. KAVIN didn't answer and he went to play with his friends. Harry was very angry with his son because his son was not obeying him. Harry thought I would teach my son a new lesson today. But first, he said, "I will drive the truck and when I come home in the evening I will teach my son a new lesson, because if I did not teach my son a lesson then he will never be able to move forward in his life." Now Harry drove the truck. It was evening and KAVIN came home. He was waiting for his father and he was very hungry. Now Harry reached home and he was so tired. KAVIN yelled at his father, "I'm so hungry give me some food." 'Harry told his son that there was only a little food left in our kitchen that only

I could eat because I was too tired to work. "And you don't eat today, go to sleep without eating." KAVIN got very angry at his father and said "why can't I eat? I am very hungry." father replied, "If you are so hungry, do for me what I say." KAVIN obeyed and asked what to do. father said, "Bring the stuff that I have put in my truck and you put it here." When KAVIN looked at the truck, he saw that it contained a lot of heavy goods. Then KAVIN told his father, "There's a lot of heavy goods in the truck that I can't carry." Harry said, "I don't know how you will carry these heavy goods. I just need these things in my room." KAVIN was very upset but he was also very hungry and he started carrying those heavy things. Harry was watching his son how he would carry all these heavy things. After some time, KAVIN was very happy when he put all those heavy things in his father's room.

Then KAVIN asked his father "now can I take my dinner". Harry was overjoyed, he hugged his son, and said, "Look, my son, what do you get by working hard?" KAVIN replied to his father, "You gave me food just by working hard."

Father replied, "if you keep working like this in your life, you will get everything. And when I work hard, then I make money, and we can eat. Otherwise, if I don't work, where will the food come from?" KAVIN answered his father, "I understand now and from today I will obey all your words and work hard and I will help you in your work." Harry said, "You are my good son, now Let's take dinner I am also hungry and go to bed early." KAVIN asked his father "why you say lie to me, there was only a little food left in our kitchen". HARRY replied "I wanted you to make you understand the meaning of hard work first. Only then could I eat well". KAVIN was happy for the first time and then they both took dinner happily. KAVIN went to sleep in his room.

Two years later, KAVIN's father became ill. And there was nothing left to eat in their home because Harry hadn't been to work in a long time. KAVIN asked his father "Do you feel hungry? Would you like something to eat? Then From today, I will go to work for you." Father replied, "You can't do what I do because it's too hard and you don't know how to drive a truck." KAVIN replied, I can do this, not for myself but for you, because until yesterday you make money for me, but today I will make money for you. And from today I will work and you will rest." The next day, KAVIN went on track for the first time. After a few days, KAVIN learned to drive a truck. KAVIN went to work all day and didn't sleep at night because he studied all night, and KAVIN also took care of his father and made food for himself and his father. One day KAVIN saw, someone was knocking on his door. KAVIN hurried out and saw two strange men calling his father.

KAVIN asked the two men, "Tell me why are you calling my father?" The two men replied that both of them had come for the loan. KAVIN said, "What kind of loan are you both talking about?" The two men replied that your father had taken from both of us. KAVIN became very upset. He told the two men, "You have been patient for a few days, and I will pay your loan." The two men replied, "We will only wait for five days. If you do not pay our loan by then, we will be forced to take your truck." Then the two men left. KAVIN thought he wouldn't tell his father because he would be upset if i told him this thing. Harry called his son and asked, "who is at the door?" KAVIN lied to his father that he was talking to himself and there was no one at the door. "You don't pay attention here and there, you need rest." The father said, "I am resting, and now you go to your room." KAVIN went to his room and he thought that if he didn't pay these two people, then they would take my father's favorite truck with them. He wouldn't let that happen, and he only had five days left. It was morning and KAVIN got ready and went to work. KAVIN went to see that two men who came to his house, and KAVIN asked the two men that how much money he would have to pay. These two men replied that you would have to pay two lakhs. KAVIN couldn't believe it. He replied, "I don't have two lakhs." The two men said, "We can't do anything, you have three days left. And if you don't give us two lakhs, we will have to come to your home again or we will have to call the police." KAVIN got upset and he had only three days left and he could not manage 2 lakhs in those three days. KAVIN went home and sat upset in his room. Harry went to KAVIN's room and his son was sad. Harry sat down behind to his son and said, "Why are you upset?" KAVIN got up quickly and said, "No, I'm not sad, why do you feel I am upset?" Harry replied "I am your father If I will not understand your pain. Who else will understand"? KAVIN lied to his father again that he had a headache so he was upset.

Father said, "If you have a headache, I'll massage your head." KAVIN replied "There is no need for that. I will rest for a while, and you too can rest in your room." Harry said, "It's okay to take care of yourself."

There were only two days left then. And KAVIN couldn't manage 2 lakhs.

And that two men came to KAVIN's home again and said, "Did you manage the money?" KAVIN replied,

"Please forgive me, the money has not been arranged yet. Please be patient." The two men got angry and they both started talking. Now they couldn't be patient anymore. They needed money quickly. KAVIN said, "How can I do it so quickly? I just do a little work that gives me a little bit of money to feed my father, and what can I do now?" The two men replied "We can't do anything. We don't care what you do. We need money till tomorrow." KAVIN asked a lot of people for help but no one helped him. KAVIN hurried to his home and went to his room and there was a small box in which he had deposited money but that money was also very little. KAVIN was very tense because he couldn't do anything. It was morning and KAVIN went out. He saw from a distance that the two men were coming towards his house. The two men reached KAVIN's house and shouted at him from a distance that we had to take your truck today because we had no other way until you gave us money. We should take your truck with us. The two men took the truck with them and KAVIN was very sad that he could not do anything. "KAVIN thought about what he would answer his father and how he would feed his father where the money would come from, what I should do now". Then KAVIN thought he shouldn't give up like that. He had to get his father's favorite truck back, no matter what he had to do. KAVIN started working hard and he studied day and night. Then, he wanted to bring back his father's favorite truck. KAVIN started working as a laborer and with the money he earned, he made food for his father and brought some things for the house.

One day, Harry asked his son, "Where's our truck for such a long time? Have you put it somewhere else?" KAVIN lied to his father for the third time, "Yeah I keep our truck in a safe place, don't worry and you relax." Harry said to his son, "Oh, that's right." Then, KAVIN went to his room and started reading. A few days later, the test that KAVIN had taken was approaching. KAVIN had to work hard for that test. And today KAVIN studied hard, he took test and he passed it.

KAVIN couldn't believe it. He was so happy because he got a job. And the company in which KAVIN got the job was very big, and on the first day, the head of that company gave RS. 500,000 to KAVIN.

KAVIN hurried to the house of the two men who had taken his father's truck. He called the two men from a distance and said, "I promise myself that I will bring back my father's favorite truck. I fulfill that promise today." The two men laughed and replied, "Do you have 2 lakhs?" KAVIN replied, "Today I have not two but five lakhs and you quickly return my truck to me and take your two lakhs." The two men couldn't believe their eyes. KAVIN paid them both and took back his truck.

When KAVIN went to his father, he became very happy and he hugged and congratulated him. And he said to his son, "I am very proud of you. And now we are no longer poor." Five months later, KAVIN built a new big house. Then, they were both living happily. KAVIN started distributing money to the poor people because KAVIN wanted the troubles that came into his life, they didn't come into anyone's life.

CHAPTER FIVE

A GIRL & HER STEP Parents

A 13-year-old girl who had no one in this world, she lived in an orphanage. And the girl's name was Emma.

And Emma was a straightforward girl who was afraid to talk to everyone. One day a woman came to this orphanage. And this woman had to adopt a child. Because this woman did not have a child. And then the woman went inside the orphanage. And when this woman saw Emma, she liked Emma very much at first sight. Then she went to Emma and started talking to her. This woman said to Emma, "Dear sweet daughter, come to me." But Emma did not answer. Woman said again, "Daughter, come, do not be afraid of me." Emma began talking in a low voice, then woman hugged Emma, Then the woman asked "Daughter, can you tell me what's your name?" Emma replied in a low voice my name is Emma. This woman said, very good name, and my name is DALIYA, and from today you are my daughter and I am your mother, and you have to come to my house, and you can ask me whatever you want, and now put a little smile on your face. Emma was very happy, and she started smiling. Then DALIYA took Emma home with them. When Emma went to house with the DALIYA, she saw that the house was very big. Then DALIYA bought new clothes from the market for Emma. Emma was overjoyed when she put on the new clothes. Now DALIYA went to the kitchen and started cooking for Emma. Then DALIYA fed Emma. Emma started talking to DDALIYA, she started talking about where my new father is.? DALIYA replied' your new father will be back home in the evening. And his name is DRAVID.

It was evening and it was time for the DRAVID to come home. When DRAVID came home he saw a little girl had come to our home, he asked his wife who is she? His wife replied, she is our new daughter Emma. DRAVID become very happy and he embraced Emma. DRAVID said to Emma, "from Today you will call me Papa." And you will go to school from tomorrow. Emma will be very happy and said, ok papa.

Then DALIYA put Emma to sleep in her room. It would be morning and Emma was very happy because she had to go to school for the first time today. DALIYA told Emma, to finish your breakfast quickly and get ready for school. Then DRAVID said, my little queen come to me quickly, first hug me, then I'll drop you at school. Emma hurried to the DRAVID and hugged him. Then Emma got ready for school, and DALIYA put Emma in the car.

Emma was very happy because she sat in a car for the first time. DRAVD took Emma to school, and got her admission. Now Emma sat in her classroom. And then DRAVID told the teacher, not to leave my daughter out of school until I came here. Teacher replied it's ok and your daughter is very sweet and brave just like you. DRAVID replied, thank you, and please take good care of my daughter. Teacher said again, oh you don't worry. Emma's life was going very well. And then Emma was very happy and she had become a very capable child.

Now Emma had grown up and she loved her parents very much and could not live without them even for a minute. One day Emma was sleeping in her room when suddenly her eyes opened. She saw that there was a fire on the roof of their house. She started shouting and She called her parents. DERAVID and DALIYA rushed out of their rooms, they both said, Daughter why are you shouting? Emma shouted that there was a fire on the roof of our house. DRAVID looked out the window to see that there was a fire, and then they all hurried out of the house, and they all cried out for help. DRAVID also called the fire service, but they arrived too late, and the whole house was burn. Emma cried a lot, DALIYA and DRAVID was very upset.

Firefighters apologized to the DRAVID and said, sorry it was too late. DRAVID replied,' it's not your fault. DALIYA said, "What are we going to do now, and where are we going? All our belongings were burnt. All the money I had kept and all my jewelry were burnt."

DRAVID told his wife, "Let's see what happens. Don't get tense."

DRAVID told his wife, we would have to live in a rented house until we built our new house. Then they all started living in a rented house. Emma was very upset because all her study equipment was burnt out and she could no longer finish her studies.

And she had to buy all his new study equipment but she didn't have that much money because all the money in her house was burnt. DRAVID said to his wife, I will borrow money from my company manager and with that money we will build our new house. DALIYA said, if he doesn't give you money then what will we do? DRAVID replied, let's see what happens.

Emma was listening to her parents and she would be very upset. Emma was thinking when I had no one in this world, they both gave me a life I could never have imagined, and today they are both in trouble. Now I have to help them. Emma went to DALIYA and hugged him and said, you don't have to worry, until yesterday you both helped me a lot and you both considered me yours, and today I will help you.

DALIYA replied "You don't need to help us. You are our sweet daughter. You see, your father will take care of everything. We are back in our home. You just watch. Don't get too tense and relax. Emma said, "Am I not able to help you both?" DALIYA said, "What are you talking about? Don't you consider us yours?"

Emma said, I love you both and I want to help you so give me a chance to help. DALIYA replied, first we'll see if your papa can do something. Emma said, let's see what happens.

DRAVID went to his manager and asked him can you help me I need money. The manager said why do you need money? DRAVID, said I had to use the money to build my new house because my house was on fire. The manager said, "I had the money, but I gave it to another man. Now I have nothing to give you." DRAVID replied, please do something I desperately need money. Manager replied, I can't do anything, ask someone else. Then DRAVID got very upset.

Now DRAVID went to his wife and he told his wife, the manager did not give me money, and then his wife also became very sad. And Emma was listening to both.

Then Emma thought now I have to do something. Emma went to DRAVID and told him, papa you not to get tense, now I will do something. DRAVID said, "Daughter, what are you going to do? Don't do anything. I'll see what happens." Emma said, "What will you do now? DRAVID replied, I have a car left which my parents gave me as a and that car is the last sign of my parents now, I will have to sell that car. Emma said, you don't have to sell the car. DRAVID said, "I have no choice." Now I can't do anything.

Emma said to the DRAVID, "Papa, rest for a while." Then Emma went outside. Emma was thinking that now I can find a job so that I can earn money and then I will give that money to my father.

Emma walked into an office. The security guard there told Emma that no one was allowed inside.

Emma asked the security guard, please Let me in. I have work some important. The security didn't let Emma in, and then Emma got very angry and she started shouting, Let me in.

The manager of this office came out and he was very young, and he told the security who is shouting. Security told the manager, that there is a crazy girl here. I don't know what happened to her and she is saying that I have some important. When the manager saw Emma, he liked her very much. The manager told the security to let the girl in, I will see What's the matter. And this manager was a very noble man, he said to Emma, what's your name? And why are you upset what's the matter. Emma replied, I am Emma, and I need work in your office, because I need a lot of money and I have to help my parents. The manager said, "Why do you want to help your parents? What happened to them? They are in any trouble? Emma said her whole story. This manager told

Emma, I felt very sad when I heard your story, and they are not your real parents. Emma replied' they are not my real parents, so what happened. They loved me more than themselves and gave me the best life, now I have to help them they are in trouble today it becomes my duty. The manager replied, "I will help you and I need something in return." Emma said, "What do you want in return?"

The manager said, "I will help you first, then I will say what I want in return." Emma said what you will ask of me in return if I don't have that then what will I do. The manager said what else can you do for your parents.?; Emma said, "I can do anything for my parents. I can even die for them." And if they had my real parents in their place, I would have done the same. Manager replied, so I am William. And I love helping everyone now I am ready for your help, and I will be very happy to help you. Emma said how can I thank you and I will never forget your kindness.

Now William helped them and gave them money and then they built their new house. DRAVID and DALIYA also thanked the William. Now Emma said to William, "What do you want from me now?" William answered, "I want to marry you." Emma replied, "I can't do that. I don't want to be away from my parents. William said, but this is what I want in return. Now no matter what happens, I just have to marry you, and I think your parents will accept me definitely.

Now William went to Emma's parents and told them, I wanted to marry your daughter. Will you both agree? DTRAVID said, "It's a great pleasure for me, yes I agree." DDRAVID and DALIYA told Emma, that we have accepted this relationship and now we want you to start your new life.

Emma said but I don't want to be away from you both. DALIYA said, "One day we will have to be away from you, and we will be very happy if you are happy. Don't worry about us and accept this relationship." Emma said if your happiness is in my happiness then I will accept this relationship but I will always remember you both and I will never forget your love till I die.

Then William and Emma will get married. Then they settled down.

But Emma did not forget the love of DRAVID and DALIYA, and she would meet them sometimes.

And she always remembered them.

CHAPTER SIX

A young Girl

A beautiful and strong girl lived with her grandmother in an old house. And the girl's name was Sophia. Sophia was a very brave and strong girl, But Sophia did not go out of the house much, she stayed inside the house. And Sophia's grandmother used to make things from clay and then sell them. Sophia loved her grandmother very much, because after the death of Sophia's parents, she had no one in this world without her grandmother. One day Grandma said to Sophia, "Now I have some things made of clay, and I will sell all these things today, then I will buy new clothes for you. Sophia said, "Grandma, there is no need for that. You brought a lot of clothes for me last time as well." Grandmother said, "It's my choice. You can't stop me." Sophia said, it's ok as you wish "and I am happy with your happiness." Now Grandmother went to buy clothes for Sophia. Now Sophia was cooking and she was waiting for her grandmother. It was getting late but Sophia's grandmother had not come home yet. Sophia became very upset. Sophia thought I should go out and see where my mother had gone, Sophia got out of the house for the first time. Sophia started thinking, that this is the first time I have been out of the house, and I don't know where the way is and where I will find my grandma now. Then Sophia said, there is no time to think I have to hurry to find my grandmother. Sophia started running very. It is getting dark and Sophia has not found her grandmother yet. Sophia got very tired while walking and she sat down under the big tree, and suddenly she fell asleep. It was morning and Sophia opened her eyes and saw that she had gone too far from her home. Sophia became very upset and was very worried about her grandmother.

There, Sophia's grandmother reached home. She saw that Sofia was not there, Then Grandma thought I had to come home early. It's all my fault. I think Sophia must have gone out to look for me and I think she must have forgotten her way home, I didn't have to leave the house, now I don't know where is she it's all my fault, now what will I do, and where did I find my sweet Sophia.

Sophia was very hungry and thirsty. She saw a beautiful palace and went inside. Sophia started talking. Is there anyone here? Suddenly a woman came out of the room. The woman said, "Are you a thief and how did you get into our house without permission?" Sophia replied, no I am not a thief I have come from far away I have forgotten my way home I am very thirsty can you give me water. The woman said, "Well, that's it. Wait a minute. I'll get you some water, this woman gave some food and water to Sophia. Sophia began to thank the woman. The woman said to Sophia, "Daughter, get out of here quickly. If the landlord of this palace came and saw you there, he will scold me again."

Sophia asked why they scolded you? The woman replied, one day a girl came here and she also asked me for water like you when I went inside to fetch water, she stole our landlord's gold box. And that gold box was the last sign of our landlord's father and since then the landlord of this palace has not allowed any girl or any unknown man to come here. Sophia replied, oh I can understand. Suddenly the landlord came and he saw Sophia, then Sophia tried to run away but landlord told her to stay there, don't even try to move. Sophia said I was just leaving here I didn't steal anything I am not any thief I came here without permission and forgive me. The woman, said to landlord, that the girl was thirsty and I gave her water and nothing. Let her go.

The landlord said to the woman, "I am not asking you, so shut up? I'm talking to this girl." Sophia got angry. She said , "I'm sorry, but you can't talk like that because she's older than you. You tell me what to say and you scold me as much as you want." Don't scold this woman. When the landlord heard Sophia's words, he felt very good. And he started talking to Sophia, you are the girl who can help me because I think you are a very smart and clever girl. Sophia said what kind of help are you talking about? The landlord replied, the girl who stole my gold box you have to bring me back. Sophia said, "Is that so?" you tell me the address of this girl I will go now and take back your gold box from there.

The landlord laughed and said, "If it were that easy, I would have gone there myself and got my gold box back, but it's not as easy as you think." Sophia said, "I don't understand what you are saying."

The landlord said that the girl is a fighter and she bet me that if there is a girl like me in this world who can beat me on the field, then if I lose in this field and that girl wins then your gold box is returned but if that girl loses then all your property is mine and your gold box is also mine. And now I have found that girl, and I think it's you who will fight that girl and then my gold box was returned to me. Sophia laughed and said, "Do you think I'm a fighter who can fight anyone? I've never fought anyone and I can't do that." The landlord said, "Don't you trust yourself?" And have you ever struggled with a problem in your life and overcame? Sophia replied, "I have suffered a lot since I was a child and I have never given up and I do what I do with forethought,". The landlord said then why are you afraid, you will help me and I think you will do it, Because I have already told you, you are brave, I have recognized you from afar, that's why when I first saw you, I told you to stop and don't move. Sophia said, if you trust me so much then I am ready to help you. But I will help you when you help me too, I forgot my way home and later you will help me to go back to my house because my grandmother is there. The landlord said, "Don't worry, I will help you too." And I promise you, "Stay here tonight. You'll be ready for battle tomorrow morning." Sophia replied, it's ok I am ready.

In the morning, Sophia is ready to fight with that fighter girl. The landlord told Sofia to eat something and then get ready to go on the battle. Sophia said I will do my best to win, and I will try to get your gold box back and then I can go home. Landlord replied, best of luck and I have full confidence in you. Sophia replied, thank you so much.

There were a lot of people in a big field. When Sophia saw all these people, she became very nervous.

The landlord told Sophia don't worry, trust yourself you will win.

Sophia said let's see what happens. The fighter girl came and said to the landlord, "Have you brought a girl with you who can compete with me?" The landlord said I brought this girl with me today who is much better than you and I have full confidence in her and she is a bigger player than you. The fighter girl said let's see how this girl is doing, now we will know as soon as we enter the battle.

The fighter girl said everyone pay attention to me and listen today a girl named Sophia is going to compete with me and let's see which of us will win.

Now the game has started and everyone is very anxious to see which of the two will win. The fighter girl told Sophia to get ready to lose, because no one has beaten me till today. And the great players have fought me, but none of them have beaten me.

Sophia replied I don't know if I will be able to beat you or not but I will try, and I am confident I have never learned to give up and today I will see What can I do?

The fighter girl said, oh great confidence, still best of luck from me, and Now let's.

The fight started, the fighter girl kicked Sophia on the shoulder, and Sophia fell down. The fighter girl laughing and she said to Sofia, "I haven't done anything yet and you fell for the first time. How cowardly you are." Sophia got up and said I am not one of the losers and I am not a coward, I am my father's brave daughter. The fighter girl said if you were your father's brave daughter, you would not fall in the first.

Sophia got very angry and slapped the fighter girl and knocked her down and then said, don't say anything about my father, I am his brave daughter and I will always be. The fighter girl got up and said, I thought there is no girl in this world who can compete with me and who is braver than me, but today I saw you and you are more powerful girl than me, and indeed you are a very brave daughter of your father. And now you have won over me and I have lost. Sophia replied, "I just came to fight you at the request of this landlord and because you brought his gold box and I promised him that I would return it to you."

The fighter girl said, "Well, I have no enmity with anyone." Sophia said, "If you have no enmity with anyone, then why you stole the landlord's gold box.? The fighter girl replied, "I stole this man's gold box so that the man could find me a girl who is very brave and strong, and this landlord brought a lot of girls to fight me but they turned out to be weak, but today I got a great player that's you. And I was looking for you. Sophia said, why do you want to be a player who is very powerful.? The fighter girl said I am a police officer, and my head police officer gave me a responsibility, He told me that you have found a girl who is very brave powerful and sharp, but I could not do it, then I made this man my victim. Sophia said, "Well, that's it." But first you give the man back his gold box. The fighter girl said I will return that gold box to him and I don't need this man now I need you. Sophia said why do you need me.? The fighter girl said, "Now you will work with me as a police officer. Because this country needs girls like you. Sophia said I can't do that. Fighter girl said, why don't you want to do? You won't get it if you are the guardian of this country.? Sophia replied, I am very lucky that you told me to work but I can't stop here because I forgot my way home and I have to go back to my house there is my grandmother and I have no one else in this world without my grandma. The fighter girl said, "You don't have to worry. I will help you and you don't have to go back to your home. We found your grandmother and will bring her here." Sophia said, "How will you bring my grandmother here? How will you find her?" fighter girl replied, I promise you within two days I found your grandmother, and you just say yes once and you get ready to work with me.

Sophia said, "Well, if you promise me, then I'm ready to work with you as a police officer. Then fighter girl took Sophia home with her and then gave her food and water, and gave her new clothes and a room to live. The fighter girl told Sophia, that you have to come to the police station with me in the morning, and I will introduce you to my head officer.

Sophia said, "Okay, I'm ready." But you also promised me that you would find my grandma, and then bring my grandma here.

The fighter girl said, "I remember my promise and I will keep it. You Don't worry." And I think you're so tired you should rest. Good night. Sophia said, "OK, I'll rest, good night.

Now it was morning and fighter girl went to Sophia's room and she said to Sophia it will be morning now you get up then Sophia got up and she got ready.

Then they both went to the police station. The fighter girl went to the head officer and told him I brought a girl with me today who is stronger than me and we need her. And the girl's name is Sofia.

The head officer said, "Let me see this girl inside. What kind of girl are you praising so much?" The fighter girl called Sophia, and said you can come in. Sophia rushed in very confidently, and she stood in front of the head officer. The head officer said, "Well, that's the girl, the head officer asked Sophia, "Can you tell me something about yourself?" Sophia said, "This is the first time I've been out of my home, but when I left my house,

I forgot my way home and reached this city. And I want to go back to my home because my grandmother is there and I have no one in this world without my grandma. The head officer said well don't worry we will help you and you don't have to go home we will bring your grandmother here. Sophia said, the fighter girl said the same thing to me, and if you bring my grandma here then well, I am ready to join the police job, and I will be very happy. The fighter girl told Sophia, "We've got our team ready and now we're going to found your grandmother." Sophia replied, it's ok.

Now the fighter girl and her team were ready and they started looking for Sophia's grandmother.

The fighter girl told Sophia, you lived in a small village, or you lived in a big village. Sophia replied, that was a small village.

Then they all went to the small village. The fighter girl said to Sophia, "Now you can tell us whether we have to go for right or left.? Sophia replied, sorry I don't know. Now what can I do.

Fighter girl said, don't worry relax.

The fighter girl told her team and Sophia we should rest for a while, so that we could continue our journey again. Sophia saw a big tree and she remembered the last time she had slept under the same tree. Sophia said loudly everyone Look, there is a big tree here and the last time I was sleeping under that tree. And I think that's the way we have to go. The fighter girl said, "Let's go all. They all went so far that the Sophia saw her home from afar.

Sophia said to fighter girl Look, that's my little house. Let's go quickly. They all ran towards the house. Grandma saw Sophia and she will be very happy. She got up quickly and hugged Sophia. Sophia told her grandmother please forgive me. I thought you went out of the house and you were too late. Then I went out of the house. Grandmother said, where did you go.? Sophia told her whole story. Grandma said to Sophia "It's a good thing you get ready to work for that police officer, and I'll be glad ." Sophia said, Grandma but you have to come to that city with me and we have to leave this village. Grandma said, I am ready to come with you.

Then they all left, and then Sophia become a police officer, Then Sophia got a new house in this city and Sophia and her Grandma started living their lives happily.

9 798885 217538

Printed by Libri Plureos GmbH in Hamburg,
Germany